The Shifting Book for Viola

by Cassia Harvey

CHP173

www.charveypublications.com - print books
www.learnstrings.com - PDF downloadable books
www.harveystringarrangements.com - chamber music

I = A String   III = G String
II = D String   IV = C String

First to second positions

1

Cassia Harvey

2

3

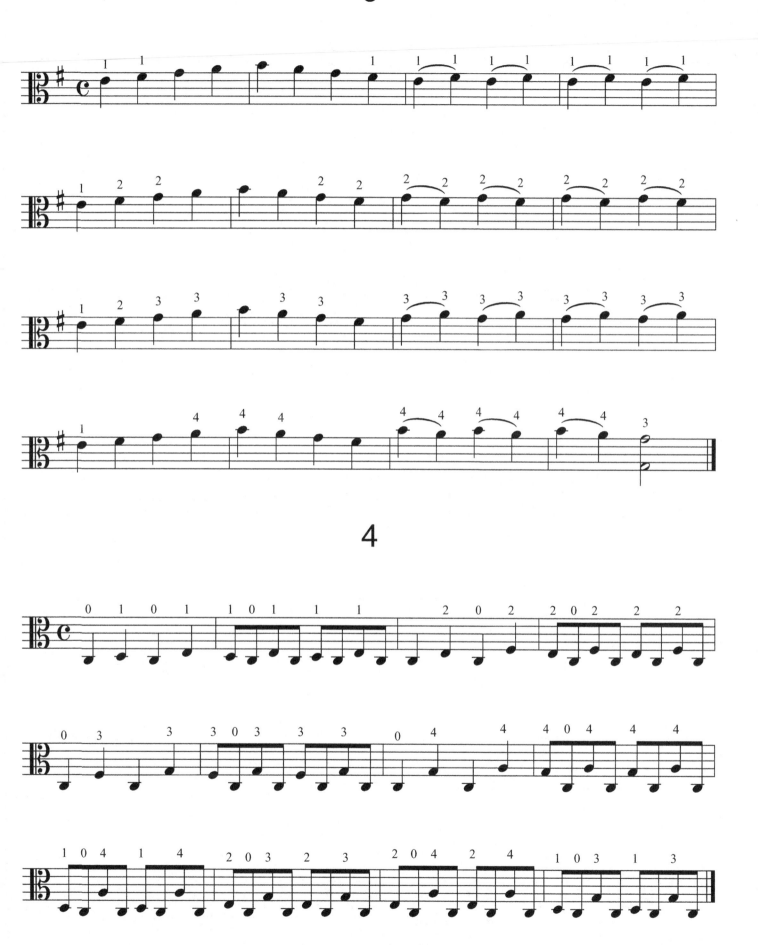

4

5

6

7

8

9

First to third positions

10

11

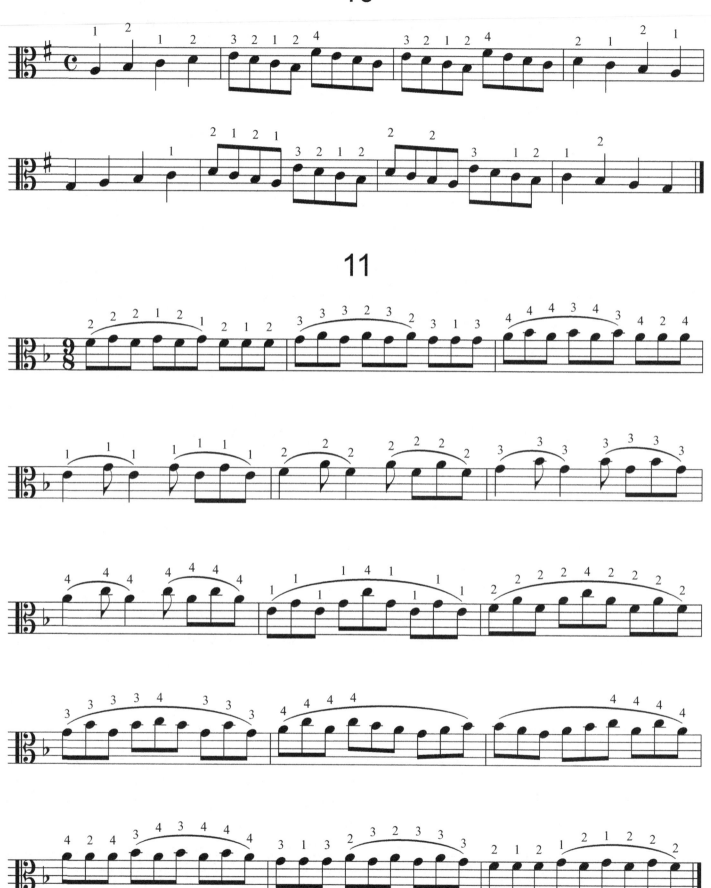

12

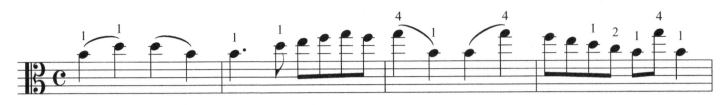

13

14

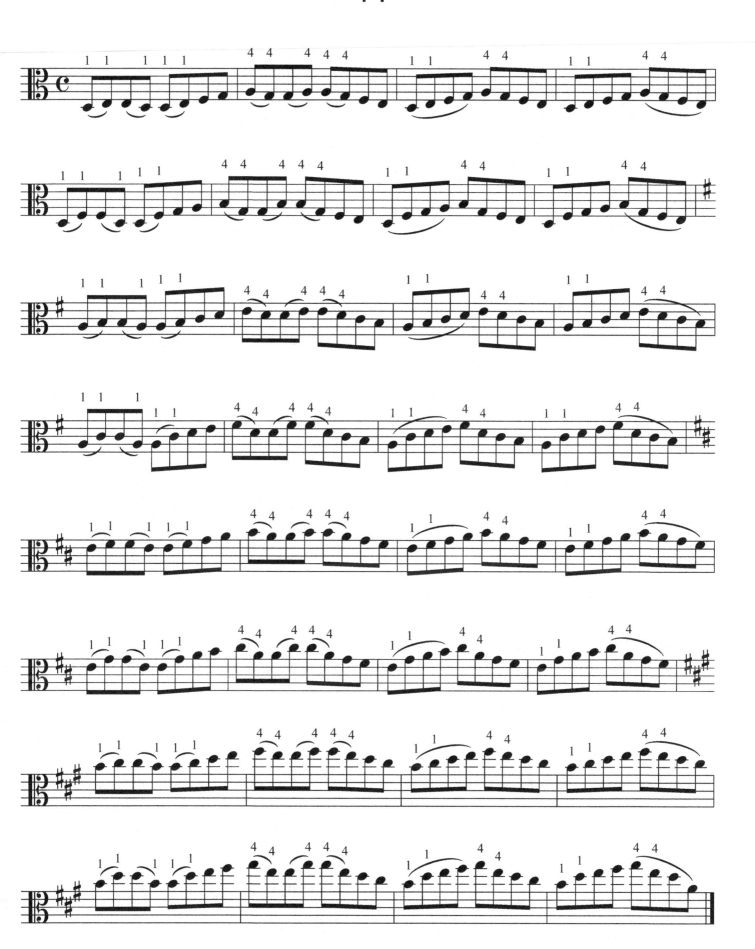

15

16

17

18

First to fourth positions

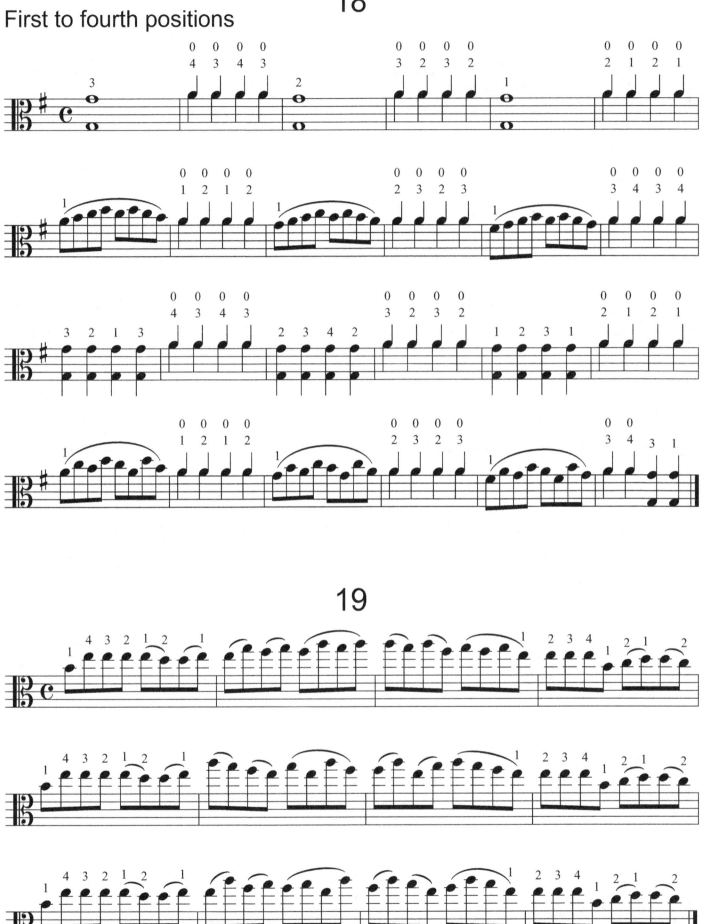

19

20

21

22

23

24

25

26

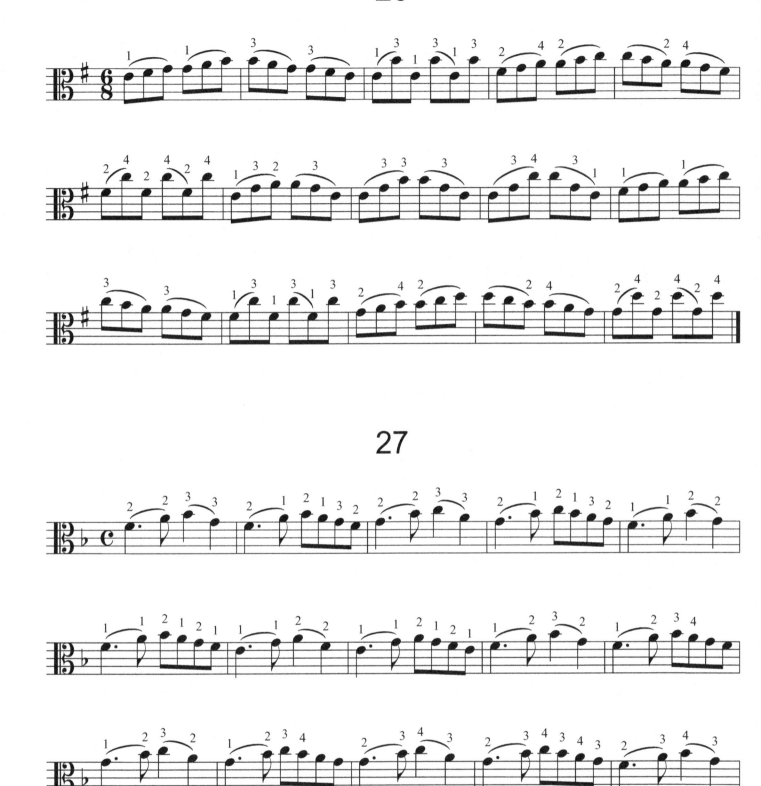

27

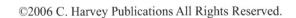

28

First to fifth positions

29

30

31

32

33

34

35

36

37

First to sixth positions

38

39

All on the C string

40

All on the D string

41

42

All on the D string

43

44

All on the D string

45

46

All on the C string

47

All on the G string

First to seventh positions

48

All on the D string

49

All on the C string

50

51

All on the D string

52

All on the D string

53

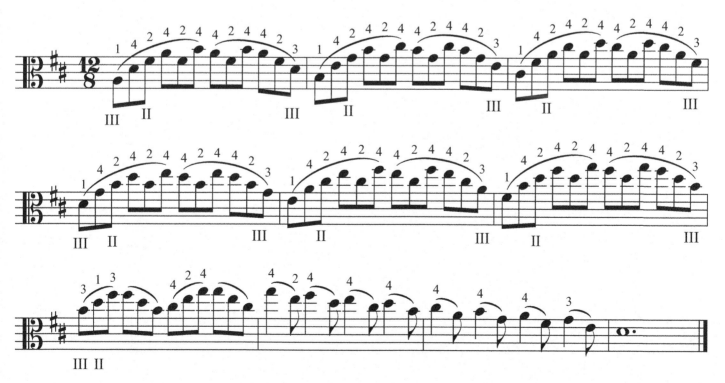

54

All on the G string

55

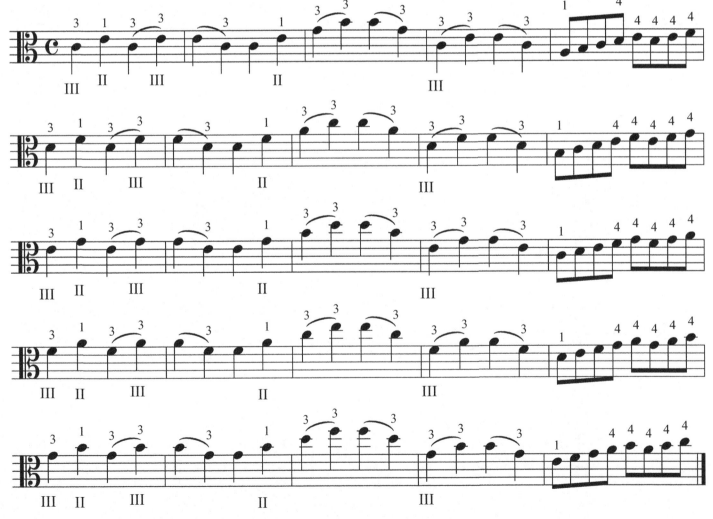

56

All on the D string

57

First to eighth positions

58

All on the D string

59

All on the C string

60

All on the C string

61

All on the D string

62

63

64

65

66

67

All on the D string

68

All on the G string

69

First to ninth positions

70

All on the D string

71

All on the G string

All on the C string

72

73

74

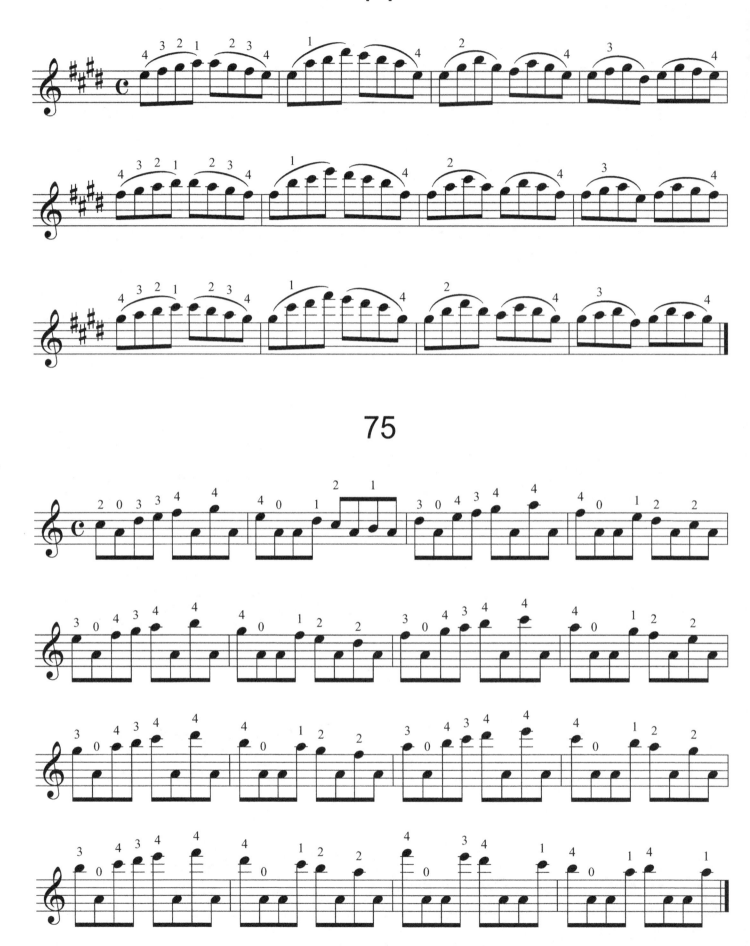

75

76

All on the D string

77

All on the G string

B♭ major

by Cassia Harvey
edited by Myanna Harvey

A string

Made in the USA
Monee, IL
03 October 2020